HAVE I MET YOU BEFORE?

LONDON STREET STYLE FROM FASHION WEEK

Photography by
Kumi Saito

2001 - 2018

Dedicated to David Yorkston

This book consists of photographs taken by Kumi Saito between 2001 - 2018;
together with comments from the journalists whom
she teamed up with at that time.
Credits are based on those at the time of the shooting.

Autumn/Winter 2017

❝ *Have I met you before?* **❞**

This is an expression that was frequently exchanged between London-based Japanese photographer Kumi Saito and the chic show-goers at London Fashion Week.

When capturing the styles of fashion insiders moving quickly from venue to venue, she was often recognised and asked *"Have I met you before?"* Or, if Kumi has photographed them before but couldn't remember who they are, she would ask *"Have I met you before?"* to which they would reply *"Ah yes, I remember you!"* and the two would start chatting. Once she gets to know them, she would continue to document their styles for many seasons. She would also cherish the opportunity and contact them when she had to photograph some inspirational looks from an icon's closet. And soon enough, her signature *"Have I met you before?"* would change to a friendly *"How are you?"*

Kumi always worked in pairs with a journalist when shooting street style photos for Japanese magazines. After she finished shooting, the journalist would write down the icon's name, occupation and details of the clothes they wore, and send that information to the magazine editors in Tokyo. Many of her photos were featured in the street style pages, alongside the best looks from Paris, Milan and New York. These pages covered not only the icons but also the latest trends from the streets, ranging from the latest must-haves, handbags, footwear and even hairstyles. The volume and amount of information on these pages were massive and considered to be equally valuable as the catwalk pages.

Japanese fashion magazines started to feature the real-life fashion moments around show venues in the early 90s. Eyeing the editors and models outside the Paris Fashion Week shows, one Japanese fashion journalist decided to pair up with a Paris-based photographer to document the best street style looks. At that time, they were the only ones taking photos outside the venues, however, it didn't take long for others to follow suit. By the early 2000s, it was obvious that the number of Japanese journalist-photographer duos had increased. We saw a significant rise in independent, street style snappers too, thanks to the digital revolution, which encouraged many photographers to shift from analogue to digital.

While street styles flourished in Paris, London was still struggling to attract influential fashion journalists, top models and celebrities. Back then, LFW was known as a showcase for Britain's young and emerging talents, while top British designers eschewed their creative home to show their collections in other fashion capitals. But surprisingly, things started to change in the late '00s. Street style coverage in magazines began to increase and rise in popularity. Moreover, Burberry made its anticipated return to LFW during Spring/Summer 2010, inspiring other brands to follow in its footsteps. All of a sudden, all eyes were on London. And LFW quickly leveled up to attract media interest and most importantly, the fashion crowd who dressed to impress the phalanx of photographers.

Kumi started shooting street style at LFW in 2001. It all began with a request from a Japanese magazine, which needed some street style photos for their hairstyle feature, as well as their shoes & handbags feature. Then gradually, she began to receive similar requests from

other magazines, and by 2008, she was shooting every season for the street style pages.

The idea of a fashion icon has evolved too. In the early '00s, fashion editors of well-known magazines were at the center of attention. British journalists, who dressed up in high heels in Paris, would dress effortlessly chic in their hometown. They were admired for their casual-meets-work wardrobes. In the late '00s, fashion buyers came into the limelight, followed by a younger crowd of fashion bloggers, who emerged from the blogging boom. Then, like in other cities, Russian It-girls became highly visible for their feminine styles, and in the late 2010s, Instagrammers and influencers started to rule the street style game.

With its powers to spread the latest news and styles across the globe easier and quicker, social media platforms, such as Instagram, have turned the heat up on the street style scene. Furthermore, it signaled the end of the Japanese street documentary tradition of pairing journalists with photographers together. It was just before we entered the year 2020.

For Kumi Saito, London Fashion Week Spring/Summer 2019 was the last season for her to capture the trendsetters outside the show venues.

Mina Wakatski
Parsnips Archive

Rebecca Lowthorpe

Elle UK

Spring/Summer 2005

Nicola Rose
Red Magazine

Autumn/Winter 2001

Harriet Quick

Vogue UK

Spring/Summer 2003

Roksanda Ilincic

Designer

Whenever I spotted someone stylish outside a show venue, Kumi would run to stop them for me, and then I would run to catch up with her. Kumi had an amazing ability to put people in a good mood. Maybe it was the way she complimented people's outfits or her charming personality, but I remember very vividly how she would always bring a smile to people's faces – even those whom she met for the first time.

Kumi had an amazing ability to put people in a good mood.

— Tomoko Kawakami —
Editor, Writer
London 1994-2002

Lara Bohinc

Designer

Spring/Summer 2002

Melanie Rickey

Editor, Consultant

Spring/Summer 2002   Spring/Summer 2005

Spring/Summer 2012

Felix Elisabetta Forma
Model, Stylist

Lucinda Chambers
Vogue UK

Sarah Harris
Women's Wear Daily, Vogue UK

Autumn/Winter 2003

Spring/Summer 2005

Autumn/Winter 2016	Spring/Summer 2013
Spring/Summer 2014	Autumn/Winter 2017
	Spring/Summer 2011

Deborah Brett

Editor

Spring/Summer 2003

| Autumn/Winter 2013 | Autumn/Winter 2018 |
| Spring/Summer 2018 | Spring/Summer 2018 |

In the early 2000s, before social media and the obsession with selfies, show venues were the easiest place to capture the best street styles in town. Why? The reason is simple: it's the place where all the fashion editors and buyers in London got together. For us, street style photography was not just about documenting the style icons. It was more about building connections with the people in the industry. For example, there is one person, whom I met while shooting people on the streets. We stayed in touch and I contacted her again when I was put in charge of a wardrobe feature, introducing inspirational outfits and accessories from people's closets. When I first met her, she was working as an assistant editor and lived in a flat with her boyfriend. A few years later, she got married and moved into a house with a garden. Then she had a baby and got promoted to fashion director. To me, Kumi's photos were special; they captured not only the best looks but also documented many people's lives.

It was more about building connections with the people in the industry.

— Miyuki Sakamoto —
Writer
London 1995-Present

Leith Clark

Vogue UK, Lula Magazine, Violet Book, Stylist

Autumn/Winter 2003　Spring/Summer 2011

Spring/Summer 2018

Arabella Greenhill
Stylist, Consultant

Spring/Summer 2005

Autumn/Winter 2016   Autumn/Winter 2017

Spring/Summer 2017   Spring/Summer 2018

Hilary Alexander
The Daily Telegraph

Autumn/Winter 2006

Isabella Blow
Editor

Autumn/Winter 2006

"

The reigning queen of street style, Isabella Blow was known for her distinctive sense of style. One time, I asked if we could shoot her wardrobe and feature them in a magazine. *"I borrow most of my clothes from designers,"* she replied. *"So, unfortunately, there is nothing worth shooting in my closet."* It's become quite common for brands to ask influencers to wear a piece from their collection to fashion week these days, but things were different back then. Isabella was way ahead of her time.

"I borrow most of my clothes from designers," she replied.

"

— Tomoko Kawakami —
Editor, Writer
London 1994-2002

Erin O'Connor
Model

Spring/Summer 2005

Spring/Summer 2017   Spring/Summer 2012

Agyness Deyn
Model

Julia Dunstall
Model

Coco Rocha
Model

Bette Franke
Model

Alice Dellal
Model

Autumn/Winter 2008

In the post-McQueen era of the mid-to-late 2000s, new catwalk stars and second-generation celebrities started to gain visibility, along with the new wave of next-gen designers. Moving into the spotlight were British It-girls, such as Agyness Deyn, Alexa Chung, Peaches Geldof, Pixie Geldof and Alice Dellal. It was the time when many photographers shifted from analogue to digital; a time before iPhones and smartphones. All the stylish and independent women at fashion week had a black BlackBerry in their hands, and they looked so cool.

Many photographers shifted from analogue to digital.

— Rumi Totoki —
Editor, Writer
London 2000-2008

Pixie Geldof
Model, Singer

Autumn/Winter 2012

Autumn/Winter 2012   Spring/Summer 2011

Spring/Summer 2012

Peaches Geldof
Model, Socialite

Autumn/Winter 2014

Bip Ling
Model, DJ, Influencer

Autumn/Winter 2011

Lulu Kennedy
Fashion East

Autumn/Winter 2011

Andrea Dellal
Model

Autumn/Winter 2011

Anna Dello Russo

Vogue Japan

Tilda Swinton
Actress

Virginia Bates
Vintage Shop Owner

Mary Portas
Retail Consultant

Spring/Summer 2011

Caroline Sieber

Stylist

Charlotte Olympia Dellal

Designer

Autumn/Winter 2014

Spring/Summer 2011   Autumn/Winter 2011

Cathy Edwards

AnOther Magazine

Autumn/Winter 2011

Sara Gilmour
Tank, Stylist

Emma Elwick-Bates
Vogue UK

Autumn/Winter 2011

Spring/Summer 2013   Autumn/Winter 2012

"

Kumi's photo sessions were always rather long. It's because she paid attention to every detail – and I mean every single detail. Even when composing her shots on the street, she would carefully adjust the way the person posed and stood in front of her camera, while looking for the best angles to show their clothes, footwear, handbags and accessories. She was very specific when it comes to backdrop too. If she wasn't happy with the background, she would usher that person to another location. It made me nervous at times, thinking that the person might get angry and walk away, but thankfully it never happened. If I were to pick one word to describe Kumi, it would be "perseverance." Street style photography is tough – it requires patience and a lot of walking – but she never gave up. Whenever a horde of photographers gathered in front of a venue to capture big celebrities, she would run straight into the crowd and keep shooting until the very last moment. Really – she was always the last one to leave.

If I were to pick one word to describe Kumi, it would be "perseverance."

"

— Miyuki Sakamoto —
Writer
London 1995-Present

Kate Lanphear
Elle US

Spring/Summer 2011

Spring/Summer 2011   Spring/Summer 2011

Spring/Summer 2011   Spring/Summer 2011

Autumn/Winter 2012

Emma Sells
Elle UK

Autumn/Winter 2011

Spring/Summer 2011   Autumn/Winter 2014

Gloria Baume
Teen Vogue

Autumn/Winter 2011

Spring/Summer 2012   Spring/Summer 2014

Taylor Tomasi
Marie Claire US, Moda Operandi

Spring/Summer 2011

Jacquetta Wheeler
Model

Autumn/Winter 2011

Jade Parfitt
Model

Spring/Summer 2011

Olivia Palermo
Socialite

Spring/Summer 2011

Alexa Chung

Model, TV Presenter, Designer

Spring/Summer 2011   Spring/Summer 2011

Autumn/Winter 2011

Autumn/Winter 2011   Autumn/Winter 2012

Autumn/Winter 2012   Autumn/Winter 2015

Autumn/Winter 2017

Valentine Fillol-Cordier
Model, Stylist, Consultant

Autumn/Winter 2011

Mario Testino • Stella Tennant
Photographer   Model

Lily Donaldson
Model

Jourdan Dunn
Model

Autumn/Winter 2011

"

During London Fashion Week, I used to sneak out of the shows before the grand finale and wait outside the entrance with Kumi, just to capture the models and their off-duty styles. Keeping abreast of emerging trends is an important part of my job and taking street style photos made it easier for me to predict the next It-model before the big-name shows in Milan and Paris. There is something special about LFW too. Compared to other fashion capitals, the overall feel is calm and relaxed. It's full of inspiration and even conversations with style icons, about their styles and what's inside their handbag, could lead to new story ideas. I also love how people mixed high fashion designer brands and vintage items. The street style scene at LFW certainly has a sense of newness and playfulness of its own.

Compared to other fashion capitals, the overall feel is calm and relaxed.

"

— Kaori Watanabe —
Editor, Writer
London 2006-2007

Clara Paget • Cara Delevingne • Suki Waterhouse
Model

Autumn/Winter 2012

Edie Campbell
Model

Autumn/Winter 2013

Hanne Gaby Odiele
Model

Poppy Delevingne
Model, Socialite, Actress

Autumn/Winter 2011

Caroline Issa
Tank

Autumn/Winter 2013

Spring/Summer 2018   Autumn/Winter 2011

Yasmin Sewell
Buyer, Consultant

Spring/Summer 2011

Spring/Summer 2014	Spring/Summer 2013
Spring/Summer 2013	Spring/Summer 2015
	Spring/Summer 2017

Tao
Model

Autumn/Winter 2011

Violaine Bernard

Feathers

Spring/Summer 2011

Yu Masui
Writer

Autumn/Winter 2013

Spring/Summer 2011

Tiffany Hsu
Lane Crawford, Selfridges, Mytheresa

Spring/Summer 2011   Autumn/Winter 2013

Spring/Summer 2014

Anya Ziourova
Tatler Russia

Autumn/Winter 2012

Irina Lazareanu
Model

Spring/Summer 2012

Tati Cotliar
Model, Stylist

Autumn/Winter 2013

Autumn/Winter 2016 Autumn/Winter 2012

Natalie Hartrey
Stylist

Spring/Summer 2011 ⋮ Autumn/Winter 2011

⋮ Autumn/Winter 2014

Julia Hobbs
Vogue UK

Autumn/Winter 2012

Caroline Rush
British Fashion Council CEO

Natalie Massenet

Net-a-Porter, Imaginary, British Fashion Council Chairman

Autumn/Winter 2011

Autumn/Winter 2014

Autumn/Winter 2017

Samantha Cameron
First Lady, Designer

Spring/Summer 2014

Natalie Kingham
Matches

Spring/Summer 2012

Ruth Runberg
Browns

Autumn/Winter 2012

"

During the golden age of fashion bloggers in the 2010s and 2011s, the front rows were filled with fresh new faces every season. Bloggers provided plenty of style inspiration back then, as many of them were mixing emerging designers with high street brands. While Kumi took their photos, I wrote down their names, occupation and all the information about what they were wearing. Needless to say, a lot of time and effort was put into the street style pages. They were so insightful; full of valuable information on the latest trends from the streets. Nothing like the street photos – on stock photo sites and social media platforms – we are seeing everywhere today.

Bloggers provided plenty of style inspiration back then. "

— Sayaka Kishi —
Editor
London 2008-2012

Susie Lau
Blogger

Spring/Summer 2011

Autumn/Winter 2012	Spring/Summer 2014
Spring/Summer 2015	Spring/Summer 2017
	Spring/Summer 2018

Julie Verhoeven
Illustrator, Designer

Hanneli Mustaparta
Model, Blogger

Nura Khan
The Sunday Times Style

Autumn/Winter 2012

Serafina Sama

Designer

Victoria Sekrier
Stylist

Spring/Summer 2012

Autumn/Winter 2012

| Autumn/Winter 2012 | Autumn/Winter 2012 |
| Spring/Summer 2014 | Spring/Summer 2014 |

I first worked with Kumi in February 2012. Little did I know that I would be working with her for many years to come. Despite the hustle and bustle of fashion week, Kumi seems to always find a way to enjoy herself. *"It's a celebration that only comes twice a year. Let's enjoy it when we can!"* she would tell me with a big smile. While searching for people to photograph, Kumi would often go missing. One time, I found her watching a show. Another time, I caught her engaged in a long conversation and even missed out on the opportunity to photograph one of the style icons. When that happens, I would call her name *"Kumi-saaaan!"* to grab her attention. Kumi can be quite spontaneous like that, but she is known to get the job done well too. When a popular celebrity, like Alexa Chung, appeared in front of a venue and immediately got surrounded by a swarm of paparazzi, she came to me and say *"Don't worry, I photographed her already"* which took me by surprise.

Kumi seems to always find a way to enjoy herself.

— Nao Koyabu —
Stylist, Coordinator
London 2012-2018

Rosalind Jana

Blogger

Autumn/Winter 2012

Marianne Theodorsen

Blogger

Somerset House brings back a lot of good memories. Back then, it was the home of London Fashion Week. It was the place where I witness the shift from bloggers to Instagrammers. The place where I would spot a new influencer, who would become so popular and impossible to photograph by next season. *"No one photographed her last season,"* Kumi and I would say to each other, feeling proud to have photographed her before anyone else. It was the best place for me to develop an eye for trends.

"No one photographed her last season," Kumi and I would say to each other.

— Nao Koyabu —
Stylist, Coordinator
London 2003-2018

Ella Catliff

Blogger

Leandra Medine
Blogger

Spring/Summer 2013

Natalia Alaverdian
Harper's Bazaar Russia, Stylist, Designer

Miroslava Duma

Buro 24/7

Spring/Summer 2013

Daria Shapovalova

FW-daily.com, More Dash

Spring/Summer 2014

Elena Perminova
Model

Emma Elwin
Elle Sweden, Stylist

Spring/Summer 2013

Tallulah Harlech
Stylist, Actress, Consultant

Autumn/Winter 2013

Spring/Summer 2013

Adwoa Aboah
Model

Autumn/Winter 2017

Spring/Summer 2013

Daisy Lowe
Model, Actress

Autumn/Winter 2014

Spring/Summer 2015

Angela Scanlon
TV Presenter

In London, local editors and socialites had their own unique styles. Some of them didn't go to Paris Fashion Week, so we were only able to capture them at LFW. I just loved the way they mixed local designer brands with vintage and high street brands. These icons were mostly spotted outside the show venues of Simone Rocha and Molly Goddard, so while watching their shows, I would get excited and think *"I wanted to photograph her! Then her next!"* And after the shows, I would run straight to Kumi and wait for them to come out.

I just loved the way they mixed local designer brands with vintage and high street brands.

— Nao Koyabu —
Stylist, Coordinator
London 2003-2018

Jefferson Hack
Dazed Media

Spring/Summer 2014

Carine Roitfeld

Harper's Bazaar, CR Fashion Book

Justin O'Shea · Veronika Heilbrunner

Mytheresa   Harper's Bazaar Germany

Spring/Summer 2014

Sarah Andelman
Colette

Autumn/Winter 2016

Eva Chen
Lucky

Spring/Summer 2015   Spring/Summer 2015

Spring/Summer 2015

Autumn/Winter 2015

Julia Sarr-Jamois
i-D, Stylist

Kate Foley

Stylist

Spring/Summer 2015

Autumn/Winter 2015   Autumn/Winter 2017

Donna Wallace
Elle UK

Autumn/Winter 2013   Autumn/Winter 2017

Spring/Summer 2017

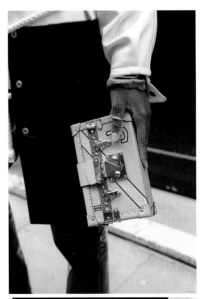

Autumn/Winter 2013	Spring/Summer 2018
Spring/Summer 2015	Spring/Summer 2017
	Spring/Summer 2017

Caroline Daur
Blogger, Model

Spring/Summer 2018

Olga Karput
Kuznetsky Most 20, Influencer

Spring/Summer 2018

Linda Fargo
Bergdorf Goodman

Spring/Summer 2018

Natasha Goldenberg

Stylist

Spring/Summer 2018

Jenny Walton
Illustrator

Spring/Summer 2017

Manami Kinoshita
Model

Spring/Summer 2017

Lisa Aiken

Net-a-Porter

Autumn/Winter 2018

Maiko Shibata
Restir

Autumn/Winter 2018

Yasmin Le Bon
Model

Karla Otto
Fashion PR

Spring/Summer 2018

"

The street style scene has changed dramatically with the rise of social media. Nowadays, anyone can call themselves a street style photographer. Whenever someone dressed in a bold, eye-catching outfit makes an entrance, people will start snapping away. Style icons have changed too. The new mix of celebrities, models and Instagrammers seem cool yet mundane, and their styles look unique yet somewhat all the same. From spotting accent colour t-shirts peeking out from jackets, to the socks-and-heels combo, or the colour-matched necklace and lipstick, it almost feels like the editor's eye for detail is no longer needed, and it's a bit sad. I wonder what kind of photos Kumi would photograph in this modern digital era.

The editor's eye for detail is no longer needed, and it's a bit sad.

"

— Kaori Watanabe —
Editor, Writer
London 2006-2007

Rina Sawayama • Naomi Shimada
Singer   Model, Activist

Spring/Summer 2018

Profile

© Shu Tomioka

Kumi Saito

Photographer, born in Yamagata Japan, 1962-2020.

After studying photography at Kuwasawa Design School in Tokyo, and working as an assistant for Minsei Tominaga and Studio Ebis, etc. she moved to London in 1994.

Her work focuses on fashion, lifestyle, portraiture and more. She was a well-known photographer who contributed to many Japanese magazines, fashion brands, department stores, and a wide range of media.

Contributors

Tomoko Kawakami
Editor, Writer
London 1994-2002

Kaori Watanabe
Editor, Writer
London 2006-2007

Miyuki Sakamoto
Writer
London 1995-Present

Sayaka Kishi
Editor
London 2008-2012

Rumi Totoki
Editor, Writer
London 2000-2008

Nao Koyabu
Stylist, Coordinator
London 2003-2018

*Listed in order of the comments appearance.

Index

Kumi Saito Photography #1

HAVE I MET YOU BEFORE?
LONDON STREET STYLE FROM FASHION WEEK 2001-2018
Photographs ©2022 Kumi Saito Archive/Aishah Sanders

Photography by Kumi Saito
Design by Maki Takizawa
Editing by Mina Wakatski
Photo coordination by Aishah Sanders, Gary Helps
English Proofreading by Reiko Kuwabara
Contributions by Tomoko Kawakami, Miyuki Sakamoto,
Rumi Totoki, Kaori Watanabe, Sayaka Kishi, Nao Koyabu
Editorial production by Parsnips Archive

Parsnips Archive
An independent publisher and creative production based in London.
Our archive team is elated to make books about fashion, culture,
lifestyle, etc. with a dedication to photography and production.
parsnips-uk.com

Published in 2022 by Parsnips Archive, United Kingdom
©2022 Parsnips Archive.

British Library Cataloguing - in - Publication Data
A catalogue copy of this book is available from the British Library

ISBN 978-1-7395963-2-3

Printed in Japan by Shinano Publishing Press Ltd.